In this dusty rear-view mirror

Also by Rodney Williams and published by Ginninderra Press
A bird-loving man: haiku and tanka

Rodney Williams

In this dusty rear-view mirror:

55 poems

with illustrations by Sally Walk

Acknowledgements

Journals in which these poems first appeared include
Antipodes, *Blackmail Press*, *Blue Dog – Australian Poetry*,
California Quarterly, *Eureka Street*, *Five Bells*,
Haight-Ashbury Literary Journal, *Kokako*, *Mascara Literary Review*,
Miriam's Well, *Overland*, *page seventeen*, *The Paradise Anthology*,
Poetry New Zealand, *Pre-Scribe*, *Tasmanian Times* and *Valley Micro-press*.

In this dusty rear-view mirror: 55 poems
ISBN 978 1 74027 936 9
Copyright © text Rodney Williams 2015
Copyright © internal illustrations Sally Walk 2015
Original cover design by Homegrown Design,
from a photo by Rodney Williams

First published 2015 by
GINNINDERRA PRESS
PO Box 3461 Port Adelaide SA 5015
www.ginninderrapress.com.au

Contents

Preface	7
The Greatest Service To Our Company	**11**
Grandpa	13
By any other name	14
Still attached	16
Roll out the barrel	18
Terms for repayment	20
Simplest lesson	22
First aid	24
Tissue	26
All the words he retained	28
The world game	29
Rocketman	30
This old church	31
Leaving Me Back Here	**33**
Animal, mineral or vegetable	35
Gertie	38
That was you	43
Half Your Self	**45**
Old stager	47
Breaking in	48
Days of concrete, blues and gold	49
Streets to the North	**57**
The car stopping outside will not be yours	59
Home first – first home	60
Veranda	61
This One That Got Away	**63**
Beyond influence	65
From Muir Woods to Walhalla	66
Landed	67
Stopper	68

A Pair of Mornings — 69
- Climate change — 71
- Not sleeping with the enemy — 72
- Fine day/storm front — 73
- Estuary breaching — 74
- High tide at midnight — 75
- Bridal party — 76
- Tetractys — 77
- Clear glass — 78
- United Flight 848 Melbourne to Los Angeles — 79

From This New World — 81
- Carmel-by-the-Sea — 83
- More gambler than pirate — 84
- Communion at San Juan Bautista — 85
- Disguises at Wawona — 87
- Departures from the Dinosaur Monument in Utah — 88
- Snapshot from Arizona — 90
- Freeze Frame from the South-west — 91
- Four-day road — 92

Despite Freedom   Never Free — 95
- Too close — 97
- Indicting Daedalus for double filicide — 99
- Portrait of the artist as a young exile — 101

Gulls Still Torch Their Hills — 103
- Yellow-tailed black cockatoos — 105
- Black Betty — 107
- Sooty oystercatchers — 108

A Dreaming Lived Hard Here — 109
- Old house – Gippsland — 111
- Gardeners — 113
- In Devonshire Lane — 115
- Point Puer — 116
- Homer Tunnel — 118
- At the Nek — 119
- Daytrip to Walhalla — 120

Preface

The fifty-five poems which make up *In this dusty rear-view mirror* have been selected from a larger body of work that has developed over more than forty years. Grouped around a range of people and places, themes and forms, moods and myths, many of the pieces offered here seek to illustrate significant relationships and experiences, a number of them viewed in retrospect.

Readers of my previous book *A bird-loving man: haiku and tanka* (2013) might be struck by considerable differences, not least in terms of the size and shape of poems featured across these two collections. The ways in which the world can be seen are, of course, at contrast too. An impulse to look backwards – in order to move forwards – is fundamental to Western poetry: 'emotion recollected in tranquillity', as Wordsworth put it. With haiku, on the other hand, the Japanese approach aims to capture a single striking moment, within the present, often via juxtaposition – directly yet suggestively; vividly but subtly.

While the minimalist strengths of haiku – not to forget the poignant lyricism of tanka – have informed my approach to writing across the last decade, I have been captivated by the leanness and immediacy of Imagist poetry since my youth. One of the poems inspired by Imagism that is included here – 'Fine day/ storm-front' – dates from 1978, when I was twenty-two years old: a dualistic viewpoint has been there all along...

If an impulse to write in lengthier genres – as well as in very short verse forms – makes me poetically bipolar, I hope that haiku purists can still find the resonance they revere in so Western a piece as – say – 'Gertie', not only set fifty years ago, but 130 lines in length, not three. Doctrines aside, I have always sought to write with heart about human issues.

While I am grateful to all editors who first published these pieces, Paul Kane (from *Antipodes*) warrants special appreciation, as does John Leonard (formerly from *Overland*). Thanks to all editors who have endorsed my work in Japanese forms too, especially Patricia Prime, Beverley George, Cynthia Rowe, Lorin Ford and Amelia Fielden.

Prompted by a compelling oil painting of the same title, the poem 'Old house – Gippsland' featured in *Rural Dwellings – Gippsland and Beyond* (2008). Thanks yet again to Otto Boron for giving me the privilege of writing that first book.

My deepest gratitude has since extended to two other visual artists. Helen Timbury's acute eye and deft hand – along with her buoyant spirit – were huge blessings with our *Bird-loving man* project. Long valued as a teaching colleague and creative collaborator, Sally Walk has since tapped into the pulse of this new collection with her fine pen and ink illustrations.

My thanks also go to Jo and Simon Griffin, from Homegrown Design, for their work in designing the cover for *In this dusty rear-view mirror*, as well as to Stephen Matthews of Ginninderra Press for his continued support of my poetry.

As an aspiring writer, while still a teenager, I appreciated advice from the late Paul Carter, and then from Ellen Kochland. Across time, James McCaughey has always been learned and acute; William Henderson, generous and erudite.

One of Australia's finest haiku poets, Jo McInerney, deserves special thanks too. Again, she has informed and affirmed this book. For years we have shared protracted phone calls and coffees, discussing a pursuit so pivotal to us both. Author of a fine book of poetry himself, another of my dearest friends – Peter Roberts – has likewise helped to steer this project; this long, slow drive: I still cherish nights spent by firesides, red wine in one hand, poems in the other…

Members of the Baw Baw Writers' Network have made a

difference: Jeannie Haughton, Tanya Dawes, Janet Marsh, Bill Frew, Jennifer Fell, Olive Lyon, Geraldine Burrowes, Carol Campbell, Kathie Olden and the late Lisa Demos.

My most heartfelt appreciation extends to kindred souls Anne Outhred and Vaya Dauphin – each in their own ways – for great belief and endorsement. Further support has come from Linton Rousseau, Kathy Meikle, Penny Asselineau, Guy Dimmick, Kate Driscoll, Jill Thompson, Iain Colquhoun, Cherie Kilpatrick, Russell Moyle, Martine Batt, Edwin Batt, David Ballantyne, Ian Outhred, Todd Cook, Ricky Allan, Steve Wiegerink, Jai Law, Kay Frost and Mark Braddick.

My sister Bronwyn and brother in-law Mark both back my writing, as did my late mother Hazel and sister Janet. Other family folk Alistair Wilson, Penelope Wilson, Pam Williams, Sue Heron, Loretta Millar, Laura McCarthy and Vincent Long have supported this work too. As for my brother David – 'bye, old pal: it breaks my heart you could not hang on long enough last winter to hold this book in your hand, come autumn.

Yet the deepest of all my thanks must go to my wife Meg, and to our children Rohan and Sophie. All three have remained brave and honest, perceptive and affirming, good-humoured and patient, even when I become precious about my latest creation. This English-teaching, poetry-writing father could not be prouder of his son and daughter for each excelling in their postgraduate studies in Chemistry and Physics. Nor could I be more grateful to their mother for fostering a passionate commitment to enquiry in both of our offspring. And so, my darlings, this third book of my life – looking into a dusty rear-view mirror, back across that life – is lovingly inscribed to each of the three of you.

In memory of my brother David, 1946–2014

With love to my wife Meg,
and to our children Rohan and Sophie

difference: Jeannie Haughton, Tanya Dawes, Janet Marsh, Bill Frew, Jennifer Fell, Olive Lyon, Geraldine Burrowes, Carol Campbell, Kathie Olden and the late Lisa Demos.

My most heartfelt appreciation extends to kindred souls Anne Outhred and Vaya Dauphin – each in their own ways – for great belief and endorsement. Further support has come from Linton Rousseau, Kathy Meikle, Penny Asselineau, Guy Dimmick, Kate Driscoll, Jill Thompson, Iain Colquhoun, Cherie Kilpatrick, Russell Moyle, Martine Batt, Edwin Batt, David Ballantyne, Ian Outhred, Todd Cook, Ricky Allan, Steve Wiegerink, Jai Law, Kay Frost and Mark Braddick.

My sister Bronwyn and brother-in-law Mark both back my writing, as did my late mother Hazel and sister Janet. Other family folk Alistair Wilson, Penelope Wilson, Pam Williams, Sue Heron, Loretta Millar, Laura McCarthy and Vincent Long have supported this work too. As for my brother David – 'bye, old pal: it breaks my heart you could not hang on long enough last winter to hold this book in your hand, come autumn.

Yet the deepest of all my thanks must go to my wife Meg, and to our children Rohan and Sophie. All three have remained brave and honest, perceptive and affirming, good-humoured and patient, even when I become precious about my latest creation. This English-teaching, poetry-writing father could not be prouder of his son and daughter for each excelling in their postgraduate studies in Chemistry and Physics. Nor could I be more grateful to their mother for fostering a passionate commitment to enquiry in both of our offspring. And so, my darlings, this third book of my life – looking into a dusty rear-view mirror, back across that life – is lovingly inscribed to each of the three of you.

In memory of my brother David, 1946–2014

With love to my wife Meg,
and to our children Rohan and Sophie

The Greatest Service To Our Company

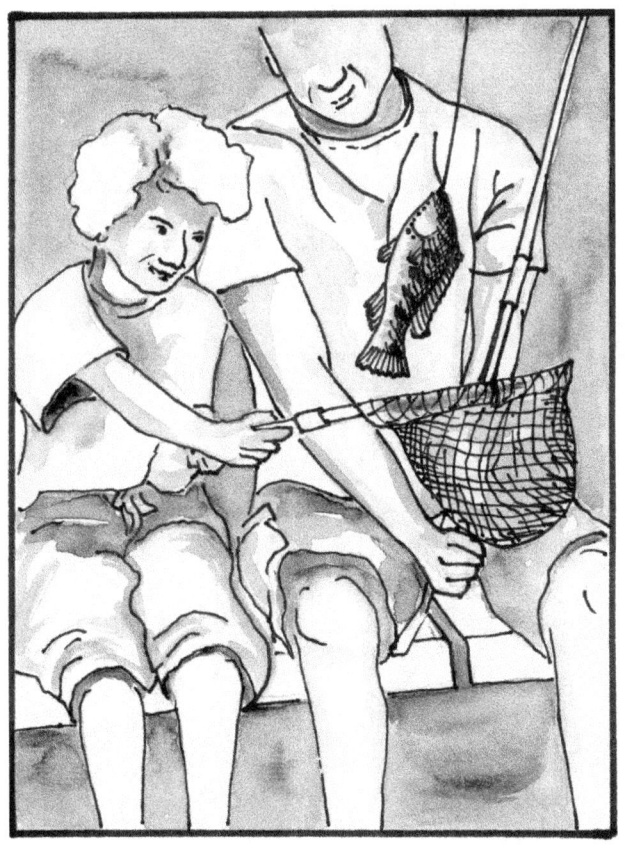

Grandpa

for my grandfather Seymour

> *oh my luve's laik*
> *a reid, reid rose*

my father's
father used to slur
in his affected brogue
fresh from his local
pub away from home

yet Grandma
tall and severe
would shrug him off
the nimblest waltzer
in the valley
left to foxtrot
with a mop

later she might soften
though, to lift
the piano lid
and favour him
with an air

> *oh Danny Boy*
> *it's you, it's you*

By any other name

for my father Bernie

Vernon

>   the name inked onto his record of birth –
>   a slip of the ear by the midwife

Bernard

>   the summons to which he'd answer
>   both magistrate and mother

Pun

>   but no play on words: his own side of the family
>   had him share an uncle's nickname – some high regard too

Big Fella

>   so dubbed by his brothers – six foot three inches tall
>   he'd stand you a beer, sling you a quid, loan you a yarn

Big Ears

>   Jughead, Wingnut, Elephant: my brother could never forget
>   he'd been promised a father – found a rival instead

Father

>   all that I could ever call him, face to face –
>   his daughters, my sisters, the same

Mud Guts

>   when he'd come home at last, Mum would find his wallet empty –
>   wine flagons too – plus a stray woman's shoe in his car

Bernie

    what loss has seen us call him, since he left
    for good – a decade later, he left this world

    he's been dead twenty years, yet still today
    for all my love I just can't say

Dad

Still attached

for my uncle Stan

you farmed windswept land
                          at Yanakie
your ridge a narrow bridge
                          between two inlets –
after the war, it put the why
                          back into anarchy,
an isthmus
            that kept Wilson's Promontory –
our southernmost tip –
                          linked to Gippsland
like a miniature Tasmania
                          still attached

emus grazed there wild
                          with your Jerseys
as a kangaroo bounded off
                          the bonnet of my father's ute
out on the Prom Road
                          after yet another night of beers

the Big Fella –
            your younger brother –
he was bound elsewhere himself though
                          for Eden in fact:
for a garden
            paradise I never quite found

as fond of a laugh

                as all your brothers

smooth across the dance floor

                        like your father

a voice as true in song

                as both your daughters

spinning forehands crosscourt

                      like their mother

blue as Corner Inlet

                your eyes like no others:

isthmus uncle

            you swelled a tide

in the inlets

            of a young man's heart –

gave me back a father's family

                    still attached

Roll out the barrel

for my uncle Len

when my uncle returned, a prisoner
of war from Changi,
he had to be carried from the troopship
at Port Melbourne – no burden,
less than half his fighting weight,
his photo a front-page grab
for a big city daily next morning

when he was released from rehab,
friends and family met at the church hall
to welcome him home – a hero
just as a survivor: flaky, remote,
not the boy he'd once been –
yet they knew a tune that would lift him

when they played 'The Beer Barrel Polka' –
the happiest song of the war –
he exploded like a landmine,
nearly heaving
the gramophone out the window

when he visited our home twenty years on –
terse as ever at the laughter of cousins –
Mum sprinted the length of the house to silence
a wireless which played that brightest of songs

when Singapore fell, Australian soldiers
had been put into pairs, then made to lie
in rows on their backs, heads facing
outwards, feet between thighs,
best mates opposite each other

when their captors gunned one row to death,
each survivor was forced – at bayonet point –
to behead his best friend with a samurai sword
and stuff his remains in a drum,
rolling it down the ravine to the river
to the sound of wartime's happiest tune

Terms for repayment

for my uncle Wal

his strike-me-lucky chuckle
remained on lease to his son lifelong,
yet Wal's sense of humour
could go absent without leave
at a farm gate left open
by his red-haired boy, or when
Hogan's Heroes came on the TV screen:
that was not how he
remembered Stalag 17

with her dead broke in pocket
and heart, Uncle Wal loaned
his wife's sister a four-figure sum
to keep my sisters and I – welcome
guests in his cowshed, riding shotgun
on his tractor – free from a state
ward's children's home:
no rate of interest charged,
no terms for repayment set

at the grave of his wife's brother
(fellow prisoner of war –
from Changi instead)
Wal's face cracked in half
when poppies fell on rosewood –
another name on the honour roll:
this time he could pull
no loved one in need
back from the depths of a hole

within twelve months a lone bugle
played the 'Last Post' once more:
having drawn no shot
from the guard tower, Wal had thought
he'd escaped the compound,
to be picked off years later –
still middle-aged –
by a booby trap left
in the heart of his ground

Simplest lesson

in memory of my cousin Geoff

I swayed crouch-kneed as a surfer
on the tray of your dad's tractor
anxious in my pride
before saliva thick as clag
could be sucked back from my hand
by poddy calves denied
their mothers by the milk truck

you had me stretch an archer's bow
then squint down doubled barrels
on your twin-triggered shotgun
my boyhood shoulder
braced against recoil
powder pungent even now
in the nostrils of memory

together we pegged out traps on dusk
our fingers freed
from that steel-jaw snap
to slip clips onto strike-plates
sprinkled with soil
hoping no fox would deny us a pelt
or your mum's sweet rabbit stew

splicing the knot you'd taught me
to cast a barb on dark
in the dam on your creek
that we called the lagoon
I risked snags and mosquitoes
for a blackfish prize
to be content instead with an eel

grasping shifts in thought
in learning chess from you
right-angled knights and castled kings
aching with plans five moves in advance
I was slow to digest your plainest advice
to let my finger rest on a pawn
lest my queen be lost

playing pontoon purely
in our hard-nosed school
of match-betting sharps
you showed me the two-fold face of an ace
either cricket team or tennis star
in value as high as eleven
as potent or useless as one

educating a cousin kid
who stole your birthday eight years on
you made me imagine the head of a coin
hidden beneath its tail…
but with my own father gone for good
your simplest lesson proved the best:
there was no shame in just being male

First aid

our mother was superintendent
to a red cross service company –
no mere charitable collectors
her crew staffed the local blood bank
while every winter weekend
in their tin booth at the netball
they'd patch up bitumen grazes
staining knees with gentian violet
soothing sobs with reassurance

from calico we kids would fashion
slings not sipped in Singapore –
as a hearth-side cottage handicraft
we'd fabricate injuries in mâché
stiff as splints on limbs still slender
sporting wounds in livid enamel
with bones jagged in card protruding
compound fractures if not interest
money tight as snakebite tourniquets

at ambulance first-aid courses
my sisters and I played patient
well schooled in all our symptoms:
a car wrecked on the roadside
could host a training exercise –
when the fire brigade held a back burn
our mum might stage a mock disaster
with her offspring cast as victim
a role we'd each learnt all too well

father had no drinking problem
if he'd another glass to drown in –
her marriage past resuscitation
mum was made citizen of the year
likewise honoured by the queen:
filling a host of poorly paid positions
the old girl kept us kids together
the greatest service to our company
her toughest first-aid exercise of all

Tissue

        finally

                at the start

    of a summer

        gone southward

against first advice

                we tell our old darling

    deep in decline

        her eldest daughter

    our big

        sister

has died

                in middle time

    in a northern

        fall

known to us

        as autumn

    whereas down here

        in her first home

    it should have been

           spring

       from an envelope

                     addressed

by my own hand

                            months before

      no longer pouching

                   card or note

        yet still hoarded

                     in her handbag

mother's first thought

                         without weeping

          is to conjure

                         a white square

       of tissue paper

                      neatly folded

         still fresh enough

                            for use

    if too thin

                for words

too dry

          for tears

All the words he retained

in memory of Jack Long

forfeiting speech for breath
no wind left to buzz an electro-larynx
my father-in-law Jack
still won a friend among strangers
in that last home known as nursing,
his ward hosting none who were deaf
yet none who could speak
at least to one another

> he'd charm and rack his daughter
> with wry digs and sharp quips
> his pointer jabbing the alphabet
> too fast for her to parse

with a single-digit wave Jack would greet
his last new pal – a Samoan
cheeks smooth as an ocean canoe
all the words he retained
from the Pacific as well
after a stroke had swamped
that atoll in his brain
where English had planted a flag

> when at last I told Jack
> I loved him, despite his guarded heart
> his final phrase came as a handshake
> which crushed my fingers through a smile

The world game

for my son Rohan

sporting events
you call them
summoning the family
to a medley of games
humouring your sister
encouraging your mother
fair in your challenge
forever teaching
me to be a surer kick
a better dad

tall as my father
you never knew
you're still growing
ready to move
to a bigger league
no transfer fee charged
your seat always kept free
for home games

Rocketman

for Rohan

running hard in close
cheerfully grim
my toddler son
kicks fiercely
at the first of many balls
missing all but air
his leg swinging high
to straddle my shoulder
as I crouch for the catch
smiling eyeball
to foresight
cradling him dangling
to purr through copper curls

dadda's got ya, rocket man

awoken with a twitch
for a job too new
too old
unwittingly loud
in my silence
I lurch from this room
spare and sparse
the place where my son
slept the sleep
of his teens
before launching himself
on a vector
from this base oblique

still miss ya kick, rocket man

This old church

for Sophie

> *a clenching of the gut*
> *in the thin dawn light…*

    this old church
    a project
    under conversion
    its weatherboards restored
    developing out of darkness
    jacked high before haulage
    from the birth town
    of my menfolk
    to the faith school
    of you my daughter
    leaving at daybreak
    for a different state

funerals for both
my farmer grandpa
and carpenter father
were held herein
yet not here…

> at my grandfather's graveside
> I'd offered a handshake
> to a figure not sighted
> for the whole of a teen age
> but my old man turned away –
> on his deathbed five years later
> his liver failing like his will
> father vowed he hadn't seen me…

        down these knotted boards
        I helped bear his pall
        only to splinter myself
        beneath that heaviest box

while his eldest brother
bid me pull myself together
I wept for losses not yet written off —
for you my heart's girl never to meet him
just as I by his hearse ever a stranger…

      a clenching of the gut
      in the thin dawn light…

Leaving Me Back Here

Animal, mineral or vegetable

for my sister Bronwyn

on endless
are we there yet
drives without number
to gran and pa's
place by the beach
we played word games
like animal, mineral or vegetable
to while away the miles

our mother hazel drove
both car and game
with aunt god-bless-her bess
on this day our navigator
all three of us kids crammed into the back
me in the middle
with girls two years either side
the eldest janet always best read
our little wait-for-me sister bronwyn
all of six years young –
as mum would forever say –
setting us a challenge
an animal starting with L

we began with a casual safari
across the african savannah
taking potshots at lions and leopards
before jan became more dogged
citing her sister's love for cats –
okay, so not a lynx

while I hazarded a snap at a lizard
aunt bessie herself felt certain
it could not be a lemur
then haze vowed she knew for sure
it had to be a lamb –
just a shake from that straight blonde fringe

down the slopes of the andes
from llamas we descended
to pests and parasites
locusts and leeches

till jano felt our guesses looked lousy
making us all dive deeper
in quest of lung-fish and lobsters
lamprey and ling

while hazie wondered if her baby girl
could possibly know a baby hare
should rightly be called a leveret
auntie b hoped that this wee pet of ours
could spot the distinction
between lap-dog and labrador
making our big sister wonder
if it was all some flight of fancy
knowing how much this little one
loved her ladybirds from storybooks
more than lyrebirds or lapwings

I could parrot off no solution
whether lory or lorikeet
to win us that nod from bronnie's gold bob –
a bunch of laughing jackasses
we all had to shrug and just give up

both the older women
even our eldest sister too
have since taken their own last drives
down another road with no end
leaving me back here to glance
in this dusty rear-view mirror
at you our wee miss thrilled to bits
from leaving all us big ones
each looking so white-faced…

for that animal starting with an L…
why, albino, silly me

Gertie

for my brother David

back in the credit-squeeze early sixties
our nineteen-thirties Dodge
had no vintage vehicle appeal
outside our clan
at best an old jalopy
in the eyes of all those
around the town
with a curl to their lips
as well as their forelocks
more often to them just a heap
of shit

our mother dubbed her Gertie
one good old girl
to another

our beloved Dodge sedan
had external headlights
perched like coastal beacons
atop her sweeping mudguards
their curves resolving
into running-boards
that no shotgun sidekick
bootlegging mobster
security jack
or cop in pursuit
would ever ride in motion
beyond imagination

black as the depression
that cast her block
she hid her engine
beneath butterfly
bonnets on either side
while her doors
hinged back and front
would swing open hard
from the centre of the car
when met by any breeze

suicide doors
they came to call that design
a full-frontal rush of air
meeting the car with highway force
mum doing all of forty-five
measured as miles
one back door sprung open
by a curious hand
that met no restraint
the jet of wind wrenching
my kindergarten body
straight onto the roadway
where I dived head-first
into a darkened ward
an oncoming driver
barely missing my death
as I bounced across bitumen

my brother ten years older
screaming no, pal, no
desperate in his lunging grab

maybe not for the last time
I'd slipped through his fingers
before he slipped through ours
leaving home young
to find work on the railways
and then in a foundry
driven out by a man
never father to him

Gert's leather upholstery
was worn cracked and cool
her backseat roomy
enough to be cramped
with sisters even cousins
on infinite drives
in summer heat
to a seaside suburb
for bedside nursing
of an ailing gran
who would beam as she winked
from eye to eye in a trice
her endless short-lived days of cancer
filled with countless memoirs
half-remembered on unending rolls
of toilet paper
deep sea scrolls of senility
while her bellyful of a husband

a former fitter-and-turner
was left free to spin
his metal in newfound lathes
where he'd no right to hold a key
for any such chuck

on Gertie's last trip
to that same long beach
on a gravel road
at a narrow bridge
another woman driver
her husband sober in navigation
drew to a halt as did our mother
with room for one car only
across that slender span
a standoff south of the border
you first – no no, you, my dear
our father chuckling into the glove-box
his cooling bottle warm in the heat
our mother tenser than ever
female heads nodding then shaking
each pair of steering hands gesturing
yeah, no, you first – oh, love, but I insist
both cars slipping at once
with a great lurch into first
thump crunch tear grind
my own crown butting the seat in front
Gertrude's front right wheel
shorn clean from its axle
her electrified klaxon

blaring fit to bring winter
its high wail sounding
as if we'd foundered at sea
the old woman at the helm
of the other car wrecked
cracking skull on windshield
the blood from her forehead
trickling bright even still

old Gertie was hauled away
to be marooned in weeds
for us kids a refuge in dry dock
the silver figurehead from her prow
in full sail all the same
the horned ram leaping yet
from the once-proud Dodge
a keepsake casting
cool in my palm
an icon I lost without being asked

when grandfather had Gert
carted off to the tip
it was yet another way that dear old pop
could make his decisive turn of hand
at the lathe of another
seem apt but not fitting

That was you

was that you, by god, after thirty years
outside a roadhouse where I bought
flowers for mother's day?
she's passed on since, but your old girl
she was gold, paying me to mow her lawn
a chore that you refused

hell, that must have been you, the kid who held
the biggest parties of boyhood
with ice cream soft-drink spiders fizzing
and a slot-car set that filled a room –
once you rolled your billycart down our hill
right beneath a reversing truck

by jesus, that was you for sure
my drinking buddy of underage teens
in our fathers' footsteps
staggering arm in arm down the milky way –
when first busted for dope, you employed no counsel
expecting a bond, amazed by conviction

that was you, by christ, still with pixie-point ears
sizing me up with a squint
you'd learnt doing time inside –
your nephew told me years and beers ago
how he'd gone to a brothel on a footy trip
only to find your wife, his aunt

for god's sake, that was you, off to your car
and I hate myself now for not calling your name

Half Your Self

Old stager

This grand old stager, he filled many a part
as lead or as a cameo of note,
yet he never quite learnt his own script by heart.

Hungry for life outside his own, from the start
cosmetics gave masks, costumers a coat:
this grand old stager, he filled many a part.

When a pup he was seen as a vain upstart –
reviews he'd recite, not afraid to gloat,
yet he never quite learnt his own script by heart.

In living many lives, he lived one apart –
passionate in role but in truth remote:
this grand old stager, he filled many a part.

To be tolerated now, a frail old fart
well past his peak – some were happy to note –
he had never quite learnt his own script by heart.

In old age less clear on what was real or art –
years since playing lover merely by rote –
this grand old stager had filled many a part,
yet he never quite learnt his own script by heart.

Breaking in

breaking in

                    sharp new boots
                    a showroom engine
                    that fractious colt
                    our boom recruit

breaking in
        on

                    delicious indiscretions
                    a scrambled parting
                    mortified silence
                    remote control reverie

breaking in
        to

                    padlocked premises
                    a bouncing jog-trot
                    spontaneous song
                    tearful applause

breaking in
        two

Days of concrete, blues and gold

memories of the Albion Hotel, Carlton

1

thrashing power chords   chopped and chunky
tremolo aching   bent notes wobbling
as he sharpened his axe   with slide riffs
ripping up the summer night   on Faraday Street
the bottleneck blues right at home   at this of all hotels
his band left to chug along   way behind him
down in the lower lounge   barely a support act
if ever the grandstand guitar   chose to go it alone
out on the pavement   all too much a solo

not having the remotest   control back then
no cordless guitars   in the 70s
he could soar to gasping heights   air thin as ageing hair
like that greatest of Carlton frontmen

                Jesaulenko, you beauty!
and just like Jezza   he too knew the value
of a good long lead

>   while the assembled crew
>   right out there too   yet always in
>   just gave its laconic nod

2

the boss   at best a cook   no chef, he
bragged   of learning his trade   on Bougainville
where the native boys were   buggered
literally   syphilis up the

steak-and-kidney pie
never a surprise   on his daily specials board
he'd leave a pot   chock full of kidneys
to simmer all afternoon   a stench that had you
screaming for a gag   viscous fluid steaming
alchemy outside its eon   urine distilled to gold
worse than the pub's *pissoir*   if fully clogged with butts

a loathing ever since   for offal of any genre
for the inner organs   of beasts and fowls
so relished by Joyce's Bloom

3

the child's cut-price serve
a promotion scant exploited
in this stale and smoky lounge
with its reek of flat spilt beer
with malt and hops gone sour

while regulars were mostly childless
at least while out here   drinking
one man   without a youngster
stammered such an order

soon due to collect used crockery
you sensed that you could catch him
crouched in some dim corner

when he looked up   gulping
guilt-edged insecurity   his half-price
meal half-gone   the shame in his gaze
made you feel   half your self

4

occasional visits   to the upper lounge
made by the professor emeritus   of literature heroic
lover of seafaring tales   Viking legends   Nordic myths
romance ballads   Scottish lyrics
stoutest defender of Robbie Burns
frail only in his frame
champion of old-world simplicity
no friend of the obscurantist

> *poetry doesn't have to be too damned difficult*
> *just to be good, young man!*

a tottering gait   but too proud for a cane
the soles of his slippers adhering
to carpet made sticky with spillage   velcro before its time
he'd set to his solitary meal   and seven-ounce shandy
his cutlery shaking   yet tucking in hearty
an old-fashioned mixed grill
best repast on offer   at this of all banquet halls
before breasting the fiord   on one last rising tide
in that longest   boat of all

5

ever cheery   the relief chef would smirk
as he thumped a customer's meal down
to steam on stainless steel   lasagne sagging
schnitzel singed   before he'd quip
> *there's somethin' to put lead in ya pencil, mate!*

only to leer at any female handy
> *but he's gotta 'ave someone ta write to, eh, luv?*

mindful of paradox   in his advice   if not his approach
> *hasten slowly, my lad – hasten slowly!*

the veteran bar manager   spurred by spirit
once felt rash enough   to fondle your buttock
as you bent   to clear   plates from a table

6

in the corner the performance poets gathered
an eyelid out   for their gothic gig
deep in converse   and coven
with witches   of white magic   and their warlock
junkies   or so went that night's barroom bulletin

in the city   weeks later   you chanced upon one
studying tarot   in a bookshop   she asked
if anything had been taken from you   back at the hotel
no, no, not your innocence!   not even money, no
just a sliver of fingernail?   some hair?   one blond curl
from that Afro of yours?   would they have used their own
scissors?   you wondered   with but a flicker of a grin

one long blink   she gave   at your second little jest
eyebrows plucked thin   arch in response
her lashes long and lustrous
black magic at least in mascara

if they have nothing of yours   to cast a spell with
she murmured   they'll hold no power   over you, then
her fingers stroking yours   dark forces about now   beware

been a while   she added   turning away
since you've been seen   around the scene
I quit   you sighed   since   since the stabbing
oh, that?   yeah, well, take care…

7

with closing time approaching
and bar staff bellowing   *time to go!*
the greatest of all stalwarts   *bohème authentique*
lay collapsed by the cigarette machine   today's golden
beers   and heavy spirits   protests and philosophies
cares and dreams   all crushing him   floorward
his bushranger beard   stretched across his chest
like a welcome mat   to the door
of his mouth   where the meal you'd served
had wiped its feet   and then shown the manners
to leave   a tip

8

in a bar that debated
all the big questions of the day
>   *what was essential to Sartre's essence*
>   *when the Left would gain full Marx*
all the key issues of the times
>   Australia timorous   in Timor
>   Kerr's cur   -sory sacking of Gough
one night a fight broke out
about the volume   of the juke box

strolling across Lygon Street
the first-round winner   by knockdown
paused outside Johnny's Green Room
but broke no frame   at the pool hall that evening
he met with a blade   through the kidney instead
no pot left there   to stew his piss in
his blood staining more
than police chalk   on concrete

>   while the assembled crew
>   right out there too   yet always in
>   just gave its laconic nod

Streets to the North

The car stopping outside will not be yours

you'll spring back into my day
an hour late – full of purpose
demanding action
whereas your telephone tone
was at best offhand

while I'll feel anxious
we're too fresh for annoyance –
salads tossed in backseat baskets
they'll have taken sweet time
no latte by the bay then

too late to drive there anyway
I'll fingertip another plan…
snow leopard cubs at the zoo –
rather gelati in the gardens
orchids at the conservatory

your knack with opening gambits
will take me *en passant* –
for a moment I'll be fooled
thinking surely we'd agreed
and I'd forgotten – again

your car's pulled up at last…

Home first – first home
for Meg

our bachelor landlord
                            market gardener
trots from his caravan
                            in the pumpkin shed
sporting bailing twine
                            as a belt
to pull crisp baby carrots
                            by the pallet

expert on native bees
                            breeder of terriers with pedigrees
the old chap across the paddock
                                  lets his exotic buck goat
browse on our hedge
                            his musk yet to be roused by heat

time then to fling
                            these cottage doors wide
hoist every window
                            part every blind
that sharp dawn sun
                            slants into our yard
not yet here
                     you're at home in my mind

Veranda

back up
inner streets
to the north
of my heart,
with my still
teen daughter
and score
aged son,
I chance upon
a cul-de-sac
in clear spring sun,
lingering beside
a veranda
fresh with paint,
where a quarter
century before
on my twenty
fifth birthday
I first kissed
their mother,
any tears
sheltered now
south of eaves
in an eyelash

This One That Got Away

Beyond influence

spring at these alpine springs
this creek flush with thaw
over moss-slide rocks
in a swirl to spite snags
before waterfall insistence
bemused by drought-phobics
afroth with the possible

tumbling lensed pebbles
from sandbar to bank
these deviant meanderings
breaking up into billabongs
only to stagnate in swampland
since an overflow of current
flood plain and simple

confluence beyond influence
once tributary clarity
now big-river density
silt thick as all deltas
towards sweet brackish brine
with that blue saline morph
a strait vindication

> creeks a jamboree for rain
> rivers a genealogy of creeks
> oceans a salt lick for rivers

From Muir Woods to Walhalla

for Rohan

in a fresh forest stream – headwater-clean –
our blood-folk close, in a united state,
you once spied a crawdaddy no one had seen;
in a fresh forest stream (headwater-clean)
you find fingerling trout now, kingfisher-keen,
just as your sight's clear, when kindred debate;
in a fresh forest stream, headwater-clean,
our blood-folk close in – a united state

Landed

speckled trout
several pound
a cubit long
elbow to fingertip
tail to lip
        no fishy story, this

this one that got away
from many a barb
        squirming worm
many a lure
        wobbling gleam
many a fly
        floating hoax

at last had mouthed a hook
it could not spit:

        rainbow trout
        stiff as a trophy fish
        landed by drought

Stopper

no plank remains to walk here
without deck or barroom swaying
where a grog shop once was haven
to sailors under canvas
this site now just a signpost
tilting like a cutter's mast
up a breaking wave of dune

from that shanty's front veranda
stable as a storm deck
an old salt low in spirit
might have cast a fine glass stopper
believing it a marker
buoyant as a wine cork
on the currents of his bender

beneath a dawn cut sheer as crystal
many a morning after
I retrieve that same glass stopper
long since left to tumble
in the tide churn of these shallows
pitted by grit of sand and shell
still blue-green as this bay

A Pair of Mornings

Climate change

your offshore islands
were once my coastal mountains
now under flood

Not sleeping with the enemy

when the armies of day
still trudge through the night
you can cry yourself
to insomnia

Fine day/storm front

in this my latest
                bedroom
windows face both
                      north and east:
rarely one to draw
                a blind
as a tenant –
        waking –
I know a pair
           of mornings
for the price
          of only one

Estuary breaching

shut tight as grit teeth

                        against a lip of sand

the mouth of the creek

                        can hold its breath no more –

a brackish brown tongue

                        licks the salt-blue bay

High tide at midnight

we'll build

        a bonfire

                above the neap

and stoke

        the foam

                through embers…

Bridal party

in convoy
with attendants
ahead in a hire car,
the bride sits high
behind her bouquet
alongside her father
in his showroom
quality tip truck,
white ribbons tied
across its bonnet,
Excavator
airbrushed
down its side

Tetractys

fall
to strike
light as leaf
heavy as lead
a hammer's balance between haft and head

Clear glass

come today
a clear glass
sound in base
slender in stem
elegant in shape
a gleaming surface
sparkling in stillness
filled flush to the brim
at the lip of substance
potent with promise
without overflow
crack or flaw
as a clear
glass
come today

United Flight 848 Melbourne to Los Angeles

after Jules Verne
with thanks to Janet & Mark

jets since skirt
the globe
in eighty hours,
not days:

then as now
it must have felt
this odd, though,
Phileas Fogg –

heading east across
the dateline,
we're flying overnight
towards today

From This New World

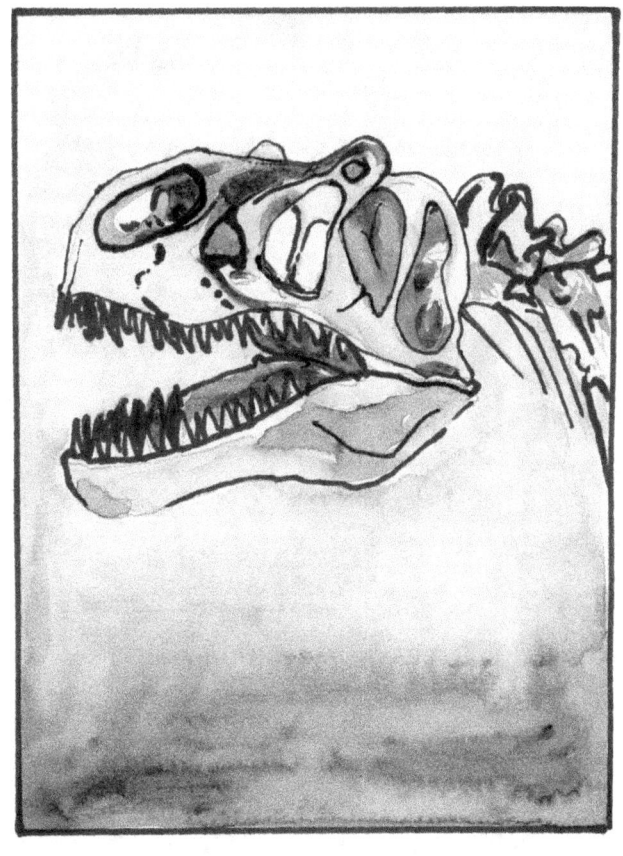

Carmel-by-the-Sea

in memory of my sister Janet

The street sign overhead read *So Carmel* –
not the abbreviation for *South*
that you'd expected:
more a superlative for local chic,
with its movie star mayor,
its coffee shops, galleries, boutiques.
One man in a tattered old shirt –
not quite *Oh so Carmel!* –
had claimed the foreshore entrance
as his beachhead.
While his children made
sandcastles around his feet,
he kept one plastic bucket spare
to remind any passing millionaire
that he ain't too proud to beg, sweet darlin',
on this coast of contradictions.

More gambler than pirate

on Seventeen-Mile Drive
millionaires have placed tollbooths
that charge for the chance
to take drive-by shots
of mansions

shielded bays
between bluffs at Point Lobos
once granted haven
to buccaneers in motion
pictures

beyond Monterey aquarium
a sea otter
floats free on its back in kelp
more gambler
than pirate

an inscrutable sharp
holding cards close to its chest
so Californian
this otter wears a starfish
as a heart

Communion at San Juan Bautista

beyond the saints

                 and saviour

past the *reredos*

                 and altar

outside the thick adobe walls

                 still whitewashed

beneath the eternal

                 depth of the shady stoops

through the clean heat of the sole

                 piazza left intact

the mission bell rings again

                 from this New World

church made old

                 built on foundations

of faith

                 by an earthquake cracked

its broken wall

                 restored

outside the square

                 a red rooster

mascot of the modern

                 village

pecks in the dust

                 beneath your feet

for a crumb

                 from your host

under the shadows

                 of antique cork-oaks

where Spanish padres

                              in times of negotiable faith

had stoppered up their dry

                                     blood vintage

back then

              their mission

                              perhaps impossible

was to convert

                native souls to

                                  Alta California

a vocation

              every bit as precious

                                        yet perilous

as any of several

                such rushes

                              for gold

Disguises at Wawona

downstream
from that captain
of all monoliths
below a basalt ridge
of Yosemite conifers
I play otter where
Merced River rapids
froth at the lip
of a swimming hole
so clear it hides
giardia's taint

gulping I dive
to a flooded beach
which harbours a fleet
of submarines
twelve to fifteen
mountain trout
all speckled as the sand
twice my depth
from alpine air
in no way tricked
by this pink-skinned bear

Departures from the Dinosaur Monument in Utah

For miles up here   rock ranges   in hue
from pink   to purple   to rust.

Across this plateau   Split Mountain
sandstone-white   yet magnetic as iron
forms a cleft peak   that lets the Green River
rise like bile   to spill   from its throat.

More a quarry   than a museum
a time capsule   disinterred
the Dinosaur National Monument
shows a pharaoh's tomb   of fossils
tilting upwards   from a swamp-bed
charnel house   of stone.

Apatosaurus bones lie   petrified as ever
despite the absence   of allosaurus
in a grave-robber's treasure trove   of claws and plates
thighs and feet   spines and skulls.

Nearby   park brochures   have trampled
a prairie dog town   right out of its ground.

Not so those petroglyphs   etched into rock   an eon ago –
a Fremont flautist   with princesses three.

Rusted signs   by the road back out
offer high desert   at steep prices
five hundred per acre   with no taker.

Into a new millennium   that flute
still echoes   off the butte.

While the prairie dogs   have left town
and even the mountain   has split
dinosaurs   confound   extinction.

Snapshot from Arizona

on easy terms with the infinite
if not with the rain gauge
new-world desert settlers
rest their mobile homes
on portable saw stools –
their foundations not yet
as concrete as planned –
heeding the scriptures' rule
not to build a house
on a bed of sand

Freeze Frame from the South-west

a
cone
of stone
old volcano
eroded remnant
long since dormant
out in this Arizona desert
now a toy top that seems to spin
while staying stock-still – a freeze frame
that flickers through the lens of the mind for miles

Four-day road

for Meg – after Joseph Boyden

our journey starts the same way it ends
crossing Canada on a four-day haul
making a united nations of friends
as elms turn gold at the start of fall

crossing Canada on a four-day haul
postcard conifers by snapshot lakes
as elms turn gold at the start of fall
an otter leaving a vee in its wake

postcard conifers by snapshot lakes
both seeing and reading *through black spruce*
an otter leaving a vee in its wake
a curl in the track towards the caboose

both seeing and reading *through black spruce*
endless beside us an eastbound freight
a curl in the track towards the caboose
that derailment of oil trucks making us late

endless beside us an eastbound freight
railhead silos on dead-flat prairies
that derailment of oil trucks making us late
Holstein cattle lined up at a dairy

railhead silos on dead-flat prairies
snowy peaks in mist through dome-car views
Holstein cattle lined up at a dairy
debate divided – elk or caribou?

snowy peaks in mist through dome-car views
a wild stream in jade beneath sheer rock
debate divided – elk or caribou?
logs chained into rafts by riverside docks

a wild stream in jade beneath sheer rock
tight hallways swaying with bunk ladders hung
logs chained into rafts by riverside docks
sorry we're late in a pair of tongues

tight hallways swaying with bunk ladders hung
making a united nations of friends
sorry we're late in a pair of tongues
our journey starts the same way it ends

Despite Freedom   Never Free

Too close

after Anthony van Dyck

too close   to his son   leans daedalus   the inventor
his breath hot   against the cheek   of this wilful stripling
the brush   of van dyck   deft across time
the free man   within the prisoner   intense
a father   ablaze with plans   if singed already
cunning in artifice   creator of a maze   to house
a minotaur   on this cretan isle   his gaol
making   and breaking   dead ends
his schemes   too fraught   for his heir icarus
this bid for liberty   flimsy   once founded
on feathers   held by string   set in wax

daedalus never a helmsman   no odysseus
stretching not sail   but wing   against wind   above water
never daring to defy   his want of a gill   no whale
his headstrong son   in dream   a gull
fleshy as a pup   barely clad   his robe oblique
backed by wings   yet no angel   out of faith
their thumbs and forefingers   each cocked alike
a boyish palm open   an older one closed
his youngster heedless   daedalus   apprehensive
vowing to fly low   tight by the tip   of father's wing
exultant as he rises   showing scant regard   instead
for earth's pull   for sun's heat   for the pitfalls   of freefall

the old man   back down there   flapping
yet the lad himself   soon lathered   sweating
blinded by glare   erratic in stroke
no no   not stalling   liquid wax burning
feathers now moulting   yes   told-you-so warnings
icarus tumbling   full-scale plummeting
first-ever sky-diver   innovative as papa
daedalus thereafter   despite freedom   never free

        one quill left floating   was since dipped   by ovid
        to scribe an ode   sparking masters   flemish
        then painters   and poets   transatlantic
        to make dead reckonings   of the azimuth
        from zenith   to horizon   towards an atlas
        mapping   fault lines   of spirit
        after icarus   had   soared
        with all that beautiful   folly   of youth
        too close   to his sun

Indicting Daedalus for double filicide

after Ovid

i) Perdix

falling
for a self-deceit
that might salve
your conscience
across the broad arch
of your exile
from greece
south to crete
daedalus
you first tossed
the son
of your own sister
to his demise
through alpine air
thin as all excuses
out of hubris
at his promise
which outstripped
your genius
precociously
inventing a saw with teeth
to cut clean through
your pride
much too bright
for avuncular vanity
your knack
with innovation

ii) Icarus

falling
for a temptation
which could soothe
your frustration
in the self-made maze
of incarceration
under minos
the despot
daedalus
you've since lured
the joy
of your own heart's pulse
to his doom too
from the heady heat
of breathless flight
exuberant
in his release
that ignored
your caution
recklessly
inspiring other youngsters
to stretch the wings
of dreams
far too bold
for paternal caution
your gift
with engineering

freeing your nephew	liberating your son
to rise up	to ascend
from the chill of bedrock	towards a solar incinerator
red-faced with blood spilt	his flight feathers plucked
as a game bird	by wax that melted
ever more	eternally
to lend his name	to share his name
perdix	icarus
to a partridge	with a sea
still bursting up slopes	still swirling as tears
beyond these stony shores	around this sorry globe

Portrait of the artist as a young exile

after James Joyce

a paradox in parable
this tale of a son
named as pater
portrayed as exile
as much as artist
expatriate across a channel
if not by air

thereafter cast as ulysses
seafaring warrior lover
questing homeward via water
as resourceful as loyal
beset by challenge
in temptation and travail
icarus but a ghost
with dedalus reincarnate
growing brash enough
to soar out of sight

first on home turf
the young sprog stephen
caned by a pedagogue
antique as any father
a christian brother
in title only
in spirit neither so
striking the upturned palm
of a hand held
level as spirit
till it quivered like a leaf
erupting into flame

the boy thereafter pledging
he would serve
neither god nor country
a land of ire
treacherous to its truest
a mother cast as sow
that could gobble her own farrow
just as flight
with a farther
daedalus had once
sacrificed a son

Gulls Still Torch Their Hills

Yellow-tailed black cockatoos

Wilson's Promontory myth #1
for the Gunai-Kurnai people of Gippsland

a thunderstorm dawn
at this time of equal night and light...
two black cockatoos
wing down from their high country
tall-tree dreaming
in feather dark as clouds over sea

>above white-capped breakers
>silver gulls wheel and squawk
>while a southerly buster
>tears away sand

their land-bound flight heavy
the cockatoos beat from shore
flexing their crests
in defence of their ground
yet no seabird's ease
rewards their pluck

>caught in a wind shift
>by the promontory's tip
>onto wave crests they're forced
>at dusk roosting in surf

borne up through night's charcoal
they find nest hollows in ashes
hatched chicks cremated
eggs baked with shells broken
ochre yolks staining
tail-feathers and crests

black cockatoos – if seen on the wing –
are sung as portents of rain:
to forsake flight might end in drought
yet gulls still torch their hills

Black Betty

Wilson's Promontory myth #2

Black Betty, settlers called her —
a fiery piece but not half bad

> on my rounds of Wilson's Promontory
> coming back from Sealer's Cove
> as park ranger I spot a hitcher
> bare skin dark as any full-blood
> her thumb more down than out
>
> I'll drop her off at Tidal River
> some decent clothes we'll find her
> no one over there she'll bother —
> as I wind down my window
> pretty Betty starts to speak

> *whitefella whalers, redhead sealers*
> *rank with blubber, sperm and steel*
> *all foul breath and sickly chests*
> *rummy heads and scabs undressed*
> *my eyes despise them still*
>
> *not enough to take our hunting*
> *they forced their way between my legs*
> *till like harpooned meat I bled*
> *then with a blade made for flensing*
> *from my trunk they docked my head*

> leaning against this ranger's truck
> I lift my noggin off my neck
> to place my block upon his bone —
> vanishing yet I haunt his sight
> as white folk vouch by campfire light

> *Black Betty, he still called me —*
> *did I send the wrong man mad?*

Sooty oystercatchers

Wilson's Promontory myth #3
for my niece Penny

>in saw-tooth bays
>on this western reach
>of Wilson's Promontory –
>Whisky Bay and Squeaky Beach
>Leonard and Norman and Oberon Bays –
>there you might still find them
>shy and elusive
>on your fringe of vision
>where an eye-tooth headland
>bites into sand:
>a pair of oystercatchers
>their sooty gleam
>a satin sheen
>arcing into view
>wheeling now in flight
>their bills scarlet spatulas
>built to shuck shells
>their pink legs
>frantic on landing
>before scuttling
>quickly out
>of sight

A Dreaming Lived Hard Here

Old house – Gippsland

after a painting by Otto Boron

topping a roll of ridge
near in distance
with ramshackle additions
of rooms at random
bleeding rust
in seepage from ceilings
dripping downwards
as a dying pulse
of bristling oil
doppelgänger for flaky enamel
the ochre of a chimney
bloody as brick
tilting with a tree
blanched in branch
anaemic against
a westerly prevailing
its trunk inclining
inviting as a girl
lithe in her teens
dancing to a tune
sung in silence
now skeletal
her blood leeched
to the root
by a forward rise
of igneous soil
friable remnant
of volcanic fire

yet no arterial flush
rich in oxygen now
to feed a dreaming
lived hard here –
a lattice
under harvest
plated in mosaic
a gridlock
towards order
the sole plaque
for aspiration
enduring

Gardeners

in the entrance
to this dim arcade
a veteran green-thumb
sets up his stall
on an ironing-board counter
made from bare hardwood
after a slow drive down
from a hilltop home
held together by vines
in order to sell pot-plants
he's struck from slips
his cut-roses long in stem
rich in scent
wrapped with a care
that cannot mask palsy

he warms to talk
of his irises
flowering abundantly
in a red-dirt field
once home to spuds
the length of its furrows
still numbered in chains
as he winks at the need
for a sprinkle of lime
around rhizomes
left bare to the sun
any varicose veins
in their sheaths of leaf
to be matched
by purple blooms

around the rim
of my own lemon tree
ripe fruit now falls
among his old bearded irises
again in bud

In Devonshire Lane

after the thirtieth anniversary of Ash Wednesday, 16 February 1983

back in devonshire lane
up on mount macedon
my old housemate's cattle dog –
allowed to lick out the porridge pot –
would opt to munch on lush green grass
in the hope of matching our boutique goat
as it pivoted on the ridge
of an A-frame hutch I'd built

the household's russet rooster
with his extravagant plume of teal
and harem of cackling bantams
would cross back-fence barbed wire
to claim provenance over forest
below the mount's memorial cross
till a fox moonlighted
as park ranger by proxy

a summer beyond our leasehold
flames seared that same slope black
on a wednesday named in ash
leaving birdsong cinder-silent there
and seventy-five dead across two states –
no tea plus scones with jam and cream
to be made again in devonshire lane
once fire had razed that roof we'd rented

Point Puer

puerile – adj. boyish, childish, immature (L *puer* boy)

carnarvon bay lies sullen
more corpse than body of water
before a stone hall blue and blackened
another century clear to heaven
retrospective in compassion
whereas convicts showing spirit
had but a ghost of a chance
as tourists through port arthur

across the brine point puer rises
its cliffs an empire's gaol for boys
where many a maiden kiss
came courtesy of the cat –
after sentences without stoppage
off to buggery youngsters went
to swirl with turnkeys and felons
down this bunghole of the world

his crime not filching snot-rags
from the nostrils of his betters
nor a gut-level misdemeanour
to wit larceny of a loaf
one lad with blood too common
was cast a hemisphere southward
from his ma's broth thin as tears
for a stunt boyish in any epoch

this youth had made a winter's trespass
on his lordship's sovereign estate
daring to skate figures free in spirit
on a lake frozen as his future –
thence barefoot without blade
he was transported to van diemens
the impact of his sport so extreme
as to shame new-age skaterboys

Homer Tunnel

blasted beneath a mountain impasse
homer tunnel swallows travellers
drawn by a milford lodestone
ground fathoms deep in granite
through a glacial imperative
before this southern island suffered
at a previous time of warming

blue as all depression
lamp-lit tunnellers thence burrowed
below stanchions now corroding
leaving nails since to rust in shale
as alpine daisies reclaim these slopes
free to bloom again untended
by any dynamiter's daughter

vagrant druids since have offered
a scatter of cairns beside this path
stonehenge reduced to bonsai
pebbles stacked as haiku
balanced in their homage
to that sheer weight of will
which presses here still

At the Nek

For men from the Australian 3rd Light Horse, killed at Gallipoli,
7 August 1915

At the Nek, three hundred lives were made nought,
their nameless remains left till after the war
within a field the size of a tennis court

That break in the ridge had strategic import,
yet Anzac plans to claim it did not transpire –
at the Nek, three hundred lives were made nought.

Destroyer shelling ceased, seven minutes short:
in that lull, to their trench the Turks retired
across a pass the width of a tennis court.

Their rifles not loaded, bearing just bayonets,
Light Horsemen on foot braved machine-gun fire –
at the Nek, three hundred lives were made nought.

Our flag reached their dug-out, went one report –
new orders to charge pushed the death-toll higher
along a front the length of a tennis court.

With losses so heavy, who would have thought
four waves of young men could be sent to expire?
At the Nek, three hundred lives were made nought
in a graveyard the size of a tennis court.

Daytrip to Walhalla

uneasy in its valley of ghosts
this gold town lives on beyond bust
graves cut steep and deep through stone
some folk buried here standing up

this gold town lives on beyond bust
its bandstand caged by scaffold
some folk buried here standing up
parrots blood-bright at feeding bowls

its bandstand caged by scaffold
lyrebirds scratching in path-side moss
parrots blood-bright at feeding bowls
weekend cabins flush with gloss

lyrebirds scratching in path-side moss
trout darting from pool to ledge
weekend cabins flush with gloss
padlocked gates on a private bridge

trout darting from pool to ledge
this creek as clear as sulphuric
padlocked gates on a private bridge
footings blown from terraced rock

this creek as clear as sulphuric
acid seeping from long-tunnel mines
footings blown from terraced rock
gravity pressing as trees incline

acid seeping from long-tunnel mines
that fire station athwart the stream
gravity pressing as trees incline
braces angled from pier to beam

that fire station athwart the stream
graves cut steep and deep through stone
braces angled from pier to beam
uneasy in this valley of ghosts

www.ingramcontent.com/pod-product-compliance
Lightning Source LLC
Chambersburg PA
CBHW070920080526
44589CB00013B/1381